Premeditated 2020

Part One
Edited and Published
By
New Look Network
20-D Amberstone Court
Annapolis, Maryland 21403
Printed by Createspace.com

Clifford8jones@gmail.com

The author and mind writer Clifford H Jones, has dedicated the words of dreams that has taken place in the past, and now, and the memory of his family in a place call America, and the Inspiration of 1776.

Table of Content

Declaration of Independence ---------- 5
(The reflection of the new world, remains)

Introduction ----------------------------------- 3

The Story ------------------------------------- 4

Words are Power -------------------------------- 5

Freedom --------------------------------------- 7

Chapter One ----------------------------------- 10

The Forthright ---------------------------------15

The Plight of Teddy ---------------------- 21

The Money Exchange ---------------------- 34

Red Square Gambling Circuit ------------ 46

The Patriotic Family ------------------------- 64

People in Power ------------------------------- 68

Poetry by the author ------------------------- 70

Introduction

The actions of moral deception that has taken place in the minds of those in the past, and now, are those as we know them. Kings with swords, and presidents with the political powers of the pen. In the world at large, we can find more of the same to fit these deceptive powers given, but are no more of a people than ourselves. The queen with wealth and quality, the prime ministers of madness, the prince with a piece of the queen's wealth that plagues the parliament, the deleterious dictators of the world, and the remains of only one true ally of the America that stands alone to protect itself. (Israel)

From the calculating congress and senate, to the supreme court of political correctness, and the weakness of decisions and opinions from these bodies that are given to us according to constitution, and Bill of rights, but have fail the people.

At some points in our time, we have given these people, the benefit of the doubt in our country, or a cheer for the better things in life because someone said, he or she can make the world a better place, but nothing, according to the people, or by the people.

We shuffle them for a period, and repetitively for decades we have given them this power. But let's not forget that the action's that have taken place in the minds of those in the past, and now, are the premeditated passages and visions of promises of change. A political gloating of political correctness and retribution of an eye for an eye. Leaders that want to inflect their powers upon us and our nation.

The timelines for all of us are structured in this premeditated fact of what we want them to be, or do, and the powers they have to satisfy our moral beliefs.

We make mistakes, and the choice to forgive or forget. But when the tragedy strikes the very core of our beliefs, the pendulum will swing with a greater risk to those that are dear to us, and their future. But the unity of family will speak with a greater power of certainty, and with a much more than just ordinary. Our goals in life are the same powers that have taken place in the minds of our past, and now, are the thoughts that gives us the same powers of achievement.

Premeditated is seldom used in the daily chatter, and if at all, it's only to identify a calculated crime of murder, and a serial killer's signature of his or her intent. The phenomenal lettering of the word itself depicts a deadly pit meeting in the minds of radical racists, a requiem of a revolutionist, and the revenge of a willful intent. A psychopathic juncture that ends for whatever reason, or purpose.

Part one of a four part series of the "Usurpation" of fact that was noted in the beginning, and set forth in the free world.   (To seize and exercise authority or possession wrongfully.) In a world of give and take, and in the words of our government, they call political correctness.

The Story

And this, the story is fiction, a generation of an American family who believes in the most powerful country in the world, and the freedoms that were born to them, whether legal or illegal.

Inspired by actual events that have taken place in cities and states across America. The names are fictional and do not reflect the lives of anyone living or dead, but crimes of retribution and greed.

Five siblings whose parents would spend their whole lives teaching them about the roads to success, and their future. Everything in their lives, and their minds had to be a beginning, and ending of a single thought. Intelligence was the goals of their professions, and everything was, and is, an expression of the freedoms, and nothing to stand in their way, or jeopardize their wellbeing.

Words are Power

Words are the only individual entity of power that we live by and the structure of our identity in any language, whether in success or failure. We are taught to identify with words and how to place the powers of convincing authority. Some believe that money is power. This, in some instances are true, but money carries a greater chance of failure for most, if the structure of words are doomed with expectations.

Our country was founded with great expectations of words from great people, and words to keep a nation safe from tyrants of usurpations.

Today we live in this 21 century in the year of our Lord and approaching the year of 2016, where the power of words have failed us, but not destroyed us, and we will again find words that will lead us to war, or the words of another leader, In God we Trust.

The Declaration of Independence

July 4, 1776, the unanimous Declaration of the thirteen United States of America, when in the Course of human events, it becomes necessary for one people to dissolve the political bands which have connected them with another, and to assume among the powers of the earth, the separate and equal station to which the Laws of nature and of Nature's God entitle them, a decent respect to the opinions of mankind requires that they should declare the causes which impel them to the separation.

We hold these truths to be self-evident, that all men are created equal, that they are endowed by their Creator with certain unalienable Rights that among these are Life, Liberty and the pursuit of Happiness. That to secure these rights, Governments are instituted among Men, deriving their just powers from the consent of the governed. That whenever any Form of Government becomes destructive of these ends, it is the Right of the People to alter or to abolish it, and to, and to institute new Government, laying its foundation on such principles and organizing its powers in such form, as to them shall seem most likely to affect their Safety and happiness. Prudence, indeed, will dictate that Governments long established should not be changed for light and transient causes, and accordingly all experience hath shewn, that mankind are more disposed to suffer, while evils are sufferable, than to right themselves by abolishing the forms to which they are accustomed. But when a long train of abuses and usurpations, pursuing invariably the same Object evinces a design to reduce them under absolute Despotism, it is their right, it is their duty, to throw off such Government, and to provide new Guards for their future security. Such as been the patient sufferance of these Colonies; and such is now the necessity which constrains them to alter their former Systems of Government. The history of the present King of Great Britain is a history of repeated injuries and usurpations, all having in direct object the establishment of an absolute Tyranny over these states. To prove this, let facts be submitted to a candid world.

Freedom

Of the many words of moral decisions that are made, and whether fact or fiction, true or false, the mind can only believe what it consumes at any given time, and identified as true or false as it is presented. A calculation of itself, and the belief of what really is, or what will be. The indications are genuine of sight and of audible belief.

We live with the abilities of our five senses. We believe that when we see something 99% is true, but with the blink of an eye, can change or verify. When we hear something, we believe that 90% is true. But there's always room for argument. The two external senses will focus to the sight of direction, and hear, to the audible belief. Our senses feed the needs for each of us every day. The life of the external sense, and the richness of the three that follow will always be, and contribute to our intelligence.

The sense of smell, taste, and feel will add to the greater needs of our decisions to guide us. They are the life line of internal circulation. The temptation of curiosity with the smell of food, and the aroma that suggest a good or bad taste of what we have become so use too. The sight of beautiful clothes and the eagerness to feel what we see.

Now that we have identified the five senses, what do we open our minds to? What we feed our bodies with each day will guide us to the richness of our destiny of what we are, and who we are. What we believe is what we see, almost all of the time. We believe what we hear, but sometimes with question. But we should always believe that none of us are perfect, we weren't meant to be, and the reasons why we have the senses to guide us to our decisions.

Well known psychiatrist have determined, after the fact, why we behave as we do, but with that, only of a statistical study.

Criminal investigators gather evidence to fact the puzzle. Today, the popular DNA, or some other findings to construct and determine a genetic structure of our identity, and sometimes finalize with an abnormal behavior relating to what may have happened in earlier years.

Can we all agree that, there are somethings that trigger's the feeding, and reaction of the sense? The alcohol we drink, and foods that don't agree to our liking. The many aromas that we inhale, many of them hold our senses accountable for our decisions.

The marijuana or cigarette smoke that filled the room that no one told you about before the party. It has been determined by medical professionals that we can get cancer being in the same room. What you believe is, did you see it? Did you hear that? Did you smell it? How did it taste? How does it feel? Our senses will trigger our lives, and with whatever form of rage or rest, and for as long as there is life itself.

They are called clicks of the senses! Something that set us off in some unforeseen direction. The life cycle is overwhelmed with the relationships of chemicals or substance that click the senses.

Scientist and medical professionals are always trying to balance the human system with exercise, good foods and chemicals, but the metabolic makeup changes in time, resulting in statistical recording in numbers of what, and time spent.

Your body's chemical intake of aromas and taste to the senses, has chosen you for the click. And as quick as you can change your mind, it can happen. This is the question so many of us have, when the spontaneous click erupts from the chemical intake in the many ways of good or bad.

Of the blind statement and words you didn't see but you heard, that insults your culture! The sense of what you heard and the headache that follows, tells you to take action. The policeman you've known for years, gives you a ticket! The college professor who teach your children, and the progression of personal attacks! Or the middle school teacher who click's with one of their students! A father that constantly beats the mother of his children, without any reasons, why?

To believe it or not, will always remain with you and the click. Many of us believe in ghosts, and some say they have seen ghost. Some of us believe in spirits that move from one body to the next, which, in some cases, have proven to be more acceptable, if you believe! If at all, and if there are supernatural powers that move in and out of our bodies with a burst of energy, we can only conclude that what we believe, are clicks of what makes us do, and a chemical reactions to things we cannot understand, and why?

They are chemical changes and not a climate change. A climate change is produced by a chemical reaction coming from the earth, because the earth is a big ball of chemicals. The habitation of the earth's people that live and survive from the chemical changes of the earth. Although, one of the smallest planets in the universe, it is vital to mankind and its chemical changes.

And for some humans in high places believe that climate change is a body that circles the earth, and has a tempered behavior that causes humans to act strange, or kill each other.

"Life can be simple, if you are worthy of existence."

Chapter One

It was the early fall of 1971 Nathan Theodore Bishop, at the age of 18 began working for General Motors as a fabricator after finishing high school. A union strong facility, UAW local 1053. He worked hard for his money, because he needed a future and for him this was the place. There were others his age and the older ones kept an eye on him, being one of the last teens that were hired. He was determined to make his future work. The union boss would always test his loyalty and work habits because he was smart, and quick to learn. He would occasionally mingle with the workers and take breaks with them. Union rules, you had to take breaks, and he was a likeable person, and got along well with others.

When he was in high school he would never let trouble find him and always one step ahead of trouble that might be developing. At the General Motors plant he would only give the company the knowledge of what he thought would give him a future.

After five years on the production line he was promoted to a senior fabricator, and supervisor. The company and union boss got to know him well, but only what he wanted them to know about him. As a supervisor he had access to the entire shop, and without question. The reason he wanted to work for General Motors was because of his mechanical ability.

He began make good money as a super, and then the word started to circulate about a strike, a walk off. He learned that you do get paid when there's a strike as long the contract is still in effect. The union wanted a new contract with better wages because the old contract was caped about to end, and he had serious concerns about his job. He had gotten to know the UB well but didn't care too much for him. He learn that strikes did happen at the plant and he didn't like it because of all the politics. He began to make his move.

Time was getting close, and the word from the UB could come at a moment's notice. It took him one day to make a pair of knuckles, one for each hand. They weren't brass but good enough for the job. The idea was to cut off the head of the lion before the strike. He wasn't very big in size, but well built at 150 pounds and able to take care of himself as he did in high school.

He knew where the UB lived, and on the second day, and ready to make his move. It wasn't political, but a force to put a freeze on what was about to happen. It was a late weekday evening, around 11:30pm, he made his way around the rear of the UB's house and made a loud noise pounding on the trash cans. The noise didn't seem to wake the neighbors and the UB didn't have any family. The lights went on and the big burley UB open the back door and stepped outside. He came straight to the trash cans where Nathan was standing in the shadows just around the corner of the house. When the UB kneeled to pick up the cans he clubbed him in the back of his head sending him to the ground. He rolled him slowly to his back making sure he was out, but not dead, and started to disfigure one side his face with the knuckles. Being careful, and not to kill him, but to send the message and taking the strike off the table. Nathan's reason was to slow the strike, and it did.

The word came the next day of what had happened to the UB and the strike was delayed. A new UB was sent in two weeks later to carry on with organizing the strike. Nathan managed to find out where he was also living and outsmarted the security. He sent the second UB to the hospital. There was never any suspicion of Nathan having anything to do with either of the UB's assaults. The plant worker's continued without incident or a contract for two months before a new contract was drawn up and finalized. The workers got everything they wanted. Nathan, in his mind was overjoyed. The union was very suspicious of GM having something to do with the attacks on the UB.

Chapter Two

Then Nathan found the love of his life. He was planning to get married while he was at the peak of his ambitions. He had known a local girl, Emma Jean Page for two years, and one day she approached him with the news of being pregnant, and with the idea of getting an abortion. Nathan was furious and told her that was about the dumbest thing he had ever heard from her. He immediately told her that she was going to have their child and that he would take care of everything. He believed in family because he was adopted. His foster parents had died, one after the other, and a year apart just after he finished high school. They were poor and living in an apartment since he was a baby, the same apartment that he and Emma Jean had shared since they met. She also had foster parents that had pasted and left her almost on the street homeless.

Before the birth of their first child Nathan started to look for a house, and found a 30 year old single family home. Made a down payment and moved in before the baby was born. The house needed a lot of work but he didn't care. He had the ability and the will. The house was a colonial and very big, with four bedrooms on the second floor, and one bath to fight over when his family starts to grow. On the first floor was a large dining area adjacent to the living room that was facing out to the front of the house. The kitchen was to the right, and behind the stairwell, and also very large. A pantry, that look like an oversized child's room was at the outside wall next to the rear outside entrance. It was deep enough, and behind a rear door in the pantry was a down stairwell to a full basement.

Nathan saw the basement as an advantage of keeping in mind that if he had to make a slight adjustment for keeping his family safe from the threats of unforeseen disasters.

Contrary to political or popular beliefs, for many years living in cook county Chicago, Illinois Nathaniel Theodore Bishop had a different outlook for his life, and his family. He was working hard to better his life, and raise a big family.

Chapter Three

In the summer of 1977 their first son was born. Nathaniel Theodore Bishop II, May 21. He was a proud father, and Emma Jean was the perfect mother. She was to be a stay at home mother and teach their children the beginnings of life.

Three years later 1980, Daniel their second son was born, and he bought an old 1973 VW for Emma Jean and the two boys to get around, and for errands.

For two years Nathan would work hard on his house every day when he came home, and on weekends. His family was growing. He had an old 1968 Chevrolet pickup that he would haul leftovers from the plant for his basement. Fabrics that were used on the production line and much of it could be used to soundproof, and waterproof a special room of the entire basement. For many years no one had ever question what he was going to do with the left over's. Some called him the junkman. Nathan didn't mine. That was the best cover anyone could ask for, and it took away any suspicions.

Nathan was getting his wishes of a big family, and on June 22, 1982 Simon their third son was born. It was after every two or three years a child was born. Michael was also a summer baby. Labor Day July 4, 1985 and the largest so far, at 8lbs 7oz. Nathan had never heard of a baby being that big.

Their last child broke the streak of a child every two or three years. Six years later Delia was born November 11, 1991, and the house was full.

Nathan believe that in his life time, the country would suffer a political uprising of protest, infrastructure burning, or nuclear disaster. He believed that by the time he retired he would have finished his room.

The Forthright

Where the family lived in Chicago, was Cook County's Hyde Park, at the near south side. An upper middle class and well developed community since the mid 1970's.

Nathan Sr. had worked a full 30 years for General Motors and the UAW local 1053, he would never forget. Keeping a watchful eye on the plant as the old guys before him retired, and the new ones coming in. He would never forget the physical adjustments he had made without suspicion.

His oldest son Nathan Jr., Teddy they called him, graduated from NYU and became a certified public accountant. Daniel finished at Illinois State University and went on to win the Heisman Trophy and play for the Chicago Bears. After eleven years, he was forced to retire with a shoulder injury. They were the only two children Nathan Sr. could put through college.

Simon, the third son won a full scholarship at UCLA, and finished at Harvard. He began teaching constitutional, and criminal law at Columbia University at NYU. Michael, the youngest of the boys was the genius. He graduated from M.I.T and went on to serve his country as an engineer in the Marines. There he became one of the high ranking commanders, of Special Forces, cyber communication, master of martial arts, and marksman. He was the best example of an American patriot of arms.

Delia, the last child and only girl of Nathan and Emma Jean Bishop, and a dazzling darling, with four big brothers, and a dream of becoming a pediatrician growing up with brothers.

When she attended Columbia University she met a graduate student. Martin Willows, they became very close and he asked Delia to marry him after he graduated. But her dreams were much bigger than marriage, and a commitment to matrimony she believed was a youth killer. Aside from just being a doctor she wanted to share some of her adult life with her mother and father, and of course, her big brothers. She did remain friends with Martin, and some day she would like for him to meet her parents. The relationship became a little distant but they still remain close friends.

Teddy grew to be much like his father. He was close to his family, and never got married. None of the boys had even come close to marriage, only Delia. They were proud of their careers. Since Daniel's retirement he became Teddy's partner. But Teddy had a ghost in his closet, and Daniel was always around.

For years gambling had become an addiction for Teddy, and quitting was nowhere in sight. He was a winner to the point of being the luckiest man on earth. The CPA business was doing well. That's how it all got started. In their partnership they set their service fees high, and that open the doors for Teddy's gambling.

If their weekends were free they would fly to Vegas. This went on for years. Teddy and his partner Daniel, in spite of the addiction, they were very resourceful for the family.

Daniel wasn't a gambler. He was a lady's man, one of the luxury's he missed as a sports hero.

2015 was almost at its end. Crime was at its peak in Cook County Chicago. Politics were on every cable channel, and so was crime. The economy was still at the top of priorities, and continued to be the worst, and remained unchanged. The people began to feel different about government. Regulations were unbearable and a trend of businesses hiring professionals to protect them from big government, and the separation of, "we the people."

The only thing left for families were a closer bonding to know who they are, and how to survive the economics and the dangers in life, and to rid themselves of any obstacles that stood in the way.

When Nathaniel Theodore Bishop Sr. retired in 2006, Teddy bought him a new pickup truck to welcome him home to rest. For thirteen years Teddy gave his parents a life of comfort that his mother and father's forest parents had never accomplished. His parents had told him their stories of foster life many times, and for him to never forgot.

Nathan and Emma Jean, and their five Siblings weren't just an ordinary upper middle class family. They were unique by choice, and much more than just American patriots. They were professionals of a well- established first blood fostered generation. A doctor, lawyer, merchants, and a chief.

When the name Nathan Theodore Bishop was ever mentioned in the city of Chicago, Teddy was the one. The one that carried the weight of the family for many years. Teddy's addiction to gambling was never a burden to the family because he wasn't a looser, but a man of winning persuasion.

The family was well aware of his problem because there weren't any secrets. What happens in the family stays in the family. Teddy was a successful CPA and business partner with his brother Daniel. And doing well for more than ten years. They had around 20 or 30 business accounts in Chicago. Their CPA charge's for each account was $6000.00 a year that included, audit, tax preparation, and certification. The business grossed about $150 to $160.000.00 a year. The only institution's that knew of the Bishop family estate's net worth was the bank, and the IRS. Teddy's winning's from gambling was kept legal as he reported it, and he made sure of that. And not a chance of anything coming back to bite him.

The family's business was managed by the sheer genius of Teddy. The family would meet four times a year at the family home. Summer's for birthdays, Thanksgiving, Christmas, and New Year, regardless of where they lived. They would call each other about 4-5 times each month, depending on the importance, or who was calling who, to establish a line of communication. The family was a well thought out family and business approach and the only way they lived. Their father and mother spent most of their life teaching their children that family would be the main structure in their lives. Teddy had gained that responsibility from his father's teachings, and the rest would except without jealousy, but with admiration and respect for Teddy, and each other. He was the executor of the Bishop Family Estate. He had setup a central banking in Chicago that was connected to his business. All earnings were produce by his brothers and sister from their professions went straight to the bank, including Teddy's winnings from gambling. Mortgage payments, apartment rentals, property taxes, utilities, phone bills, social, and business expenses. Teddy was the chief accountant who gave his family the freedom to live a life without worry, and one of the very reasons why Delia, the only girl, had never broken the family bond with or without a decision to marry. She felt that her family was a rooted system of obligation that was never for years, meant to be broken.

Like many things in life, some things will, or must come to an end. Gambling wasn't a crime if you're in the right state, and of legal persuasion. Teddy's addiction didn't show any signs of quitting. He was winning every weekend that he and Daniel could find time to visit the Los Vegas blackjack tables.

But the one time, and the only time, Teddy had miss a payoff loan to the Russians. He had never made any loans from the Russians in the past, and the Russians were the one challenge to his long streaks of winning he had to settle.

His winnings were nonstop. The casino had grown accustom to Teddy and his bouncer brother. He would buffer with deposits into transfer escrows to the casino's holding accounts. His winnings were deposited directly into the family's bank account. But the one mistake he encountered with the Russians would cost him and his family in the worst way.

Everyone knew Teddy and his brother from Chicago, even the Russians. Teddy didn't know who was Russian because no one had an accent. At least not the ones he was making a loan with.

The weekend before Thanksgiving he had bagged a little over $200,000.00 in winnings, and owed $100,000.00 to the Russians. He and Daniel had slipped out on the Russians. A big mistake! He had 48 hours to pay up. Every loan made outside of the house was a gamble on your life, and border's on illegal. Loan sharks cap their transactions at 48 hours, Teddy knows this, and so did Daniel. But they left Vegas on a flight home on a Saturday afternoon. This would mean another trip to Vegas on Monday or Tuesday to pay the Russians.

Teddy mistake went against what his father had taught him. The decision would have a rippling effect in his life and he realized he had, for the moment forgotten his father's warning. He had slipped into a moral deception and the principals of his father's teachings.

Chapter four

When Teddy and Daniel arrived in Los Vegas late Thursday afternoon, six days before Thanksgiving with the family back in Chicago. Teddy wanted to get an early start at the blackjack tables. A popular casino they would visit almost every weekend called The Blackjack. Teddy felt good, extra good about his luck because Friday the 21st was his birthday.

"Hey Danny boy, let's eat after we check in."

"Ok with me, I'm starving."

"Let's get the seafood, we had it the last time, and it was good." Teddy suggested.

"Straight up my man, and then find the ladies." Danny was worked up with his usual self.

Teddy flagged a taxi. They would always travel light on their weekend visit. Two changes of clothes and plenty of room for the money load. Daniel was his usual self, pointing at the ladies.

"Check out the ladies. Man, this is going to be one hell of a weekend."

They arrived at the hotel and casino around 7:30 pm. Teddy's mind was far from the ladies. His mission was the blackjack tables, and nothing else.

"Hey Danny, when we get there you check us in, I'll go and check out the tables then we'll get something to eat. I'm sure you won't miss me." He chuckled.

Teddy had about five grand on him, and Danny usually around two grand and change. He didn't see Danny for about an hour, and assumed he was getting something to eat. Well into another hour, and down to two grand he had struck out.

His phone was vibrating, and he looked down to see that it was his father. There was no time to talk to daddy now, so he ignored the call. He knew that he was getting a call from daddy, reminding them of Thanksgiving dinner or wishing him a happy birthday.

Danny appeared, to check in on his brother as he moved around the table to face him. Looking at him, he could see that things weren't going well. Teddy flashed him with a gesture of needing cash, and raising one finger, meant that daddy had called. Two fingers if it his mama. They only used the gestures when at a disadvantage to take the call from their parents.

Teddy liked to keep plenty of cash moving to make the dealer nervous. It worked most of the time, but he depended mostly on lady luck.

Danny passed him the cash, and hooked up with one of the casino ladies, confident that his brother would get his cash back.

The Plight of Teddy

It only took about two hands and Teddy gave a thumb up knowing Danny was somewhere close. He started to place heavy bets, and he was back down to two grand. It wasn't anything new to Teddy. He had seen this trip of losing before, and walked out with $50,000.00. To save himself from a total loss he decided to visit the casino's house business office. They knew him well from their last visit to the casino, about two weeks before. Teddy along with Danny setup a house escrow of $200,000.00 that was transferred from the family estate. Danny was at first, reluctant to do it, but eventually agreed. It was the most he had put into an escrow. Tomorrow was

Teddy's birthday and he would add another $200,000.00, and there would be no questions asked from Danny. He never doubted his brother. He left the tables for a moment and reached for his phone to call Danny. One ring and Danny picked up.

"Hey, what's up?"

"Danny, what's the room number, I'm going up."

"Where are you?" Danny asked.

"I'm at the casino office."

"Why are you there?"

"Danny, Danny stop with the questions, I'll show you when I see you, what's the room number?"

"I'll be there," said Danny.

"Why? Just tell me, I can find my way. What's wrong with you?"

He was getting very impatient, trying to understand why the room number was such a secret. Danny had visited the room and didn't want Teddy to know. He was there balling the chick Sheena he knew from the casino.

Teddy hung up and headed for the front office register to get the room number, it was 1221. It put a smile on his face. He had admitted many times being an addicted gambler with a strong belief in luck, chance, superstition, and the omen of numbers. His game was blackjack 21, and his birthday was Friday the 21st. That day would be his lucky day, five days before Thanksgiving.

When he approached the elevator, the door opened, there stood Danny with a very tall brunette clinging to him as though he was the last man on earth. A voluptuous Amazon that turned all eyes. Danny and his partner stepped from the elevator.

"There you are, I should've known," said Teddy.

"Hey Teddy, this is Sheena. Teddy's my big brother."

"Danny, how many times are you going to introduce us? Remember the last time. Grid iron hit's beginning to tell on you, little brother."

They only knew Sheena by her first name, and close relationships didn't matter in a casino. Teddy was okay with his losses and to turn it off for the night. "I'm going up to the room, you coming?"

"What, its only 10 0'clock," said Danny. The girl laughed.

"What's wrong Danny, you have a curfew?" The girl uttered with a smile.

"No, shut up bitch!" Danny whaled with a loaded quarterback sound as though he was back in the game.

She was sparked with objections to the tone, and surprised by the gaping observers. She yelled at him with the same tone, and lashed back.

"What did you say, bitch?"

"I said, SHUT UP BITCH!" repeating himself with a little more aggression.

Sheena returned the flavor. "Screw you, and your curfew daddy, bitch." She said, and stomped away.

"She called you my daddy." Said Danny.

"Geez Danny, don't you get it, curfew .... time limit," said Teddy.

"Let's get something to eat. I heard they have a great salmon entrée that's out of this world." Drawing Danny's attention away from the bitch.

Teddy's eyes were not on just Danny and his lady when she left, he had noticed two well-dressed observers, pivoting at the registration desk pointing a pistol like finger at him as they went into the restaurant. When they sat down for dinner, Danny asked. "How much did you get?"

"I bumped the escrow another 200 grand on top of the 200 we left. The house already has the account number to transfer the winnings, all I have to do is tell them when to make it. I'm not completely buster."

"Are you out of your mind?" Danny said in a much lower tone.

"I'm going to make this one, the big one my friend."

"So your plans are to hit the tables hard tomorrow," said Danny.

"Yep, start with the blackjack tables, win some cash, about 50 grand, and then switch to five card stud, much higher stake's in that game. Man, do I feel lucky."

"And when you finally answer the call from daddy, what will you tell him?"

"If he ask, I'll tell him that we are on a business trip."

"Oh that's great, lie to your father, right?"

"This is business Danny, we have to keep bumping our family business, don't you agree?"

Danny with a smile on his face said, "I wouldn't have it any other way."

"Danny, the last check on the family's worth was about 5.6 million, and that's all cash. This isn't a gamble, it's an investment. All I have to do is keep it above 400 grand. Maybe double it."

The waitress came over to the table and smiled at Danny. He returned the smile and placed the entrée Teddy suggested. Teddy ordered the same, and leaned back in his chair looking at Danny.

"Oh man, here it comes," said Danny.

"Just out of curiosity Danny, what is the room number?"

"I know that look, its 1221." said Danny.

"Do you know what tomorrow is?" Teddy asked.

"Yes, it's Friday."

"And what else?" Teddy asked.

"It's your birthday Teddy, I didn't forget. We never forget family birthdays."

"And the room number I didn't forget either. You know how I feel about these things."

They started to laugh in jubilation, and the waitress came over with their orders.

"Happiness, I love seeing people laughing and having a good time, it makes my day." She said.

As she set the food slowly on the table, they noticed her name tag said Molly.

"I see a lot of people every day but seems like it's hard for them to take little time for joy. Are you guys going to have some dessert?"

"Nope, mama didn't raise sugar daddy's." said Danny.

"Everybody loves dessert." She said.

"We're not everybody, we're somebody, just a couple of waters please." said Teddy.

They were just beginning to eat and Teddy didn't want any more interruptions. He tapped his plate to get Danny's attention. "Danny; pay the lady, and be generous."

"I'm out." said Danny with a smile.

"Yah Right!" Said Teddy, as Danny pulled out a hundred dollar bill.

"This should take care of it." He gave it to the waitress.

"You make the bill anyway you want Molly, the rest is yours."

"Thanks a heap you guys. Come back to see me real soon.

"Let's call it a night, tomorrow's a big day."

They left the restaurant and headed for the elevator. Teddy checked his watch as they arrived on the 12th floor, exiting the elevator. It was 10:45, long after Danny's curfew. Danny pointed in the direction of the room as he pulled out the key card. He quickly looked back at Teddy as though he was expecting someone. He was thinking about earlier when he and Sheena were there. He couldn't remember if they had left the room in a mess. Teddy was a very organized person and Danny didn't want to hear him ramping all night.

He opened the door and rushed in the bedroom. The suite was setup as an apartment, one bedroom, and living space. Teddy looked at him patiently, shook his head and followed. He saw a piece of white paper on the floor. He turned and picked it up. His name was on it, and read,

"Meet me in the lobby tonight at your convenience." It was signed Bobby. He remembered the two guys in the lobby, and the attention they gave him. He yelled out to Danny.

"I have to run down to the lobby, I forgot something." Danny was so busy trying to get things in order, he didn't mine at all.

Just as Teddy entered the elevator his phone buzzed. It was his father. "Hey Dad!" He answered.

"Sorry to bother you guys so late son, just wanted to make sure you don't forget Thanksgiving dinner at home. Delia will be here the day before to help her mother with dinner. My children stay so busy, and I just needed to remind you."

"Okay dad, I won't forget. I'll tell Danny, and give Simon and Michael a call. Give mama my love!"

"Sure enough, see you all then. Do what you do best son, I love you!"

Teddy heard his father loud and clear, but his mind was on Bobby. As he entered the lobby he observed a young blonde white guy around 25, one of the two he had observed earlier. He had on an oversized light green suit that stood out like a morning sunrise. Teddy assumed that this had to be Bobby.

Teddy was about to be introduced to a soldier in one of the largest crime families in the Los Vegas gambling arena. Bobby was the son of Boryenka Fedorov, a heavy hitting Russian mafia crime boss who immigrated to U.S. in the 1960's just before the Vietnam War.

Boryenka was about 30 years old at the time who over stayed his visa, and never return to Russia. He began making big money when the riots started in 1968. Illegal gambling and prostitution was his venue to make millions. When he was 35 he married a Russian woman in New Jersey that he imported from Russia to help reign in

27

his power. The couple moved to Las Vegas in 1969 and his organization was growing faster than he had anticipated. His name became familiar in the gambling circuit and his wife began to attract comrades he knew from Russia which were also illegal to live in Vegas.

In 1991 the couple had their first child, they named their daughter Sheena. And four years later their first boy, Borva Fedorov, nickname Bobby. Later when he was a teenager, he was the bully of the Fedorov family. In the late 1960's and early 1970's it was easy to come to America and get loss, and that they did. There were no questions of their children being in school, and only that the children were Russian, and welcome in name.

The children never went to college, and a fear of finding that they were anchor babies, the product of an illegal entry into America.

Sheena Fedorov, at the age of 30 was labeled the voluptuous Amazon of the gambling circuit for 5 years working the casino as a hostess, and on call for whatever would satisfy her father's wealth. Little brother Bobby, after he turned 21 worked the high volume loan business for gamblers who needed money fast, with a 10% interest on payoff returns. The sister and brother team put a long time watch on Teddy and Danny, and Bobby was about to make his move. Sheena was to keep an eye on their movements. Bobby knew that Teddy was a high stakes gambler, and could see his greed for bigger wins at any cost.

The arguments with Danny was part of Sheena's game to distance her move to a better watch. Boryenka Fedorov used his children in the worst ways, to satisfy his greed. Sheena had the looks, and sexual fortitude to do whatever it took to satisfy the family. She had the beauty of her mother, and legs to carry the almost 6ft. frame she got from her daddy, and the attention of Danny.

Teddy made his way towards Bobby, and the little runt's hands went up as though he was meeting a long lost friend from the past. Teddy extended his hand, and Bobby reached up and clutched him with a hug, moving his hands up and down his back to his waist, as though he was frisking for a weapon. Teddy remembered his last search was at the airport, and knew right away Bobby wasn't a federal agent.

"Teddy my man, how are you?"

Teddy could hear a little nervousness when the punk addressed him, but maybe because of the age difference or his inexperience.

"I'm good do I know you?" Teddy asked.

"My name is Bobby, that's all you need to know right now. I've been watching you win, but you seem to have had a little streak of bad luck."

"That won't last, you can bet on it!" Said Teddy.

"That's why I'm here. You see Teddy, I can spot a lucky man when I see one. How would you like to double, or even triple your winnings?"

"Well, I think I know how to do that, but just out of curiosity, how would you double or triple my winnings?"

Bobby was much shorter than Teddy, so he moved to his side, to see if there was anyone close to hear the conversation, and invited Teddy to a table in the restaurant. They sat at the same table Teddy and Danny sat earlier, and the same waitress came over to take their order. Molly clearly knew who Bobby was, and Teddy noticed a flushed look of confusion.

"What's wrong darling, you look like you've seen a ghost." He said.

"Oh, nothing, I just remembered you and your brother were here earlier. We're closing the restaurant soon, what can I get you?"

"Just a couple of waters, we won't be long."

Bobby pulled out a twenty dollar bill and gave it to her so she would leave. "Thank you Bobby!" she said, as she rolled her eyes in disgust.

"Looks like you lost a fan Bobby!"

"Now getting back to our business, what do you think of the offer?"

"Well, we don't have any business yet, you were telling me how I could triple my winnings."

"To the point Teddy, what if I loaned you 50 grand cash, at a 5% interest in 48 hours, and another 5% after 72 hours, can we deal?"

"Man.....you believe in me just as much as I believe in myself. Why don't we make it 100 grand cash?"

Before Bobby could respond Molly brought the water, sat it on the table, and left. He leaned over closer to Teddy.

"We can meet tomorrow around 4pm, don't look for me, set at the bar I'll come to you, 100 grand, Right?"

"Do I need to repeat myself?" Teddy snapped.

"No later than 4:30, after that, the deal's off." He said. He could see that Bobby got the message.

They left the restaurant going their separate ways. Teddy took the elevator back to his room. He knew he had to call Michael and Simon before it's too late to let them know what was going on, and what he had put up against the estate. When he entered the room Danny was flipping the TV remote.

"Hey Danny, we have to call Michael and Simon."

"Where have you been man? Sure I'll ring Mikoli first," speaking with a Russian accent.

He would always mess around with Michael, and call him Mikoli when he would return from one of his overseas trips, and visits to the American embassy in Russia. His service duties took him out of the country a lot.

Before he made the call he briefed Teddy.

"Did you know that when Michael went to Russia, Delia asked him to find Russia's smallest hand gun, and buy two for her. It was called, Hellweg Paddle, she told him it was just the right size and small enough for her hands."

"What, he told you that?"

"No, Delia told me at his birthday party when we were home. You do remember the party, right?"

"Why would she need guns like that?"

"She said, because of where she lived, and late night shifts at the hospital. If one or two ever gets stolen there wouldn't be a trace back to her."

"Your little sister believed that two choices are better than one."

"How did Michael get those guns back into the states?"

"He's armed forces Teddy. With his ranks, he can fly anywhere in the world, and armed with a weapon. Before he moved, you know he bought a new Corvette. Well, he packed his guns, and

Delia's in a duffle bag, put them in the trunk of the car. Loaded it onto a Marine C130 plane, and they flew him and his car to the base in Dover. Then he drove to Quantico, where he is now. The transport from Russia was US government official business."

"Now I know."

Michael began calling little sister DD, for deadly Delia. He says she's good, and just as good as him."

"I guess we should all feel safe with a little sister like that," said Teddy with a little chuckle.

After the second ring on Michael's cell phone he picked up. When the brother's made their calls to each other, cells were the only means of communication, and always put in a conference call, candid and coded for security. No money was discussed, and if at all, they understood the language.

"Hey little brother, are you clean?" Meaning he was alone, or at home alone.

"With a whistle," Michael answered.

"Hold on, I have to connect Simon." Danny put a speed dial in for Simon. "Hello your honor, are you decent?"

"As can be!" Said Simon.

"Michael, I hear you've got your feet on the ground!" Referring to his last trip. "Yep, and trying to hold steady."

"Teddy, are you still trying to reach the moon? Are the craters full?" Simon asked.

"Everything looks good, as a matter of fact, excellent, I'm seriously considering parking my ship and canceling all future trips."

"I wasn't even told that. Hey guys that's good news right?" asked Danny.

"We've got a celebration coming up, maybe as early as next week."

"I talk to daddy about an hour ago; he's expecting us to be there on Thanksgiving," said Teddy.

"Michael, you and the judge better get rolling, pack your bags, and mount your mares, you've got quite a trip."

Danny you've been calling me the judge for a while now, what's your point?" Simon asked.

"Come on judge, don't you get it? You've made a reputation for yourself in New York, and everyone knows you in Chicago. Now it's time for an appointment to the bench, don't you think? Maybe even here in Chicago, it's your home, right? Here's my wish, Clarence Thomas is about to retire, Maybe President Washington would love to have you as the replacement. Your name has got to be out there. That's my dream for you brother, you deserve it."

"Amen to that!" said Teddy.

"Well, it doesn't exactly work like that, but I do have good news fellows. Sometime ago I decided to become a congressman to represent the state of Illinois"

"That is good news!" Said Teddy.

"That was years ago, and you are just now telling us! We are into the presidential elections." Said Danny.

"I've been wanting to break the news, but I was going to do it after the presidential elections."

"Does daddy know this? He keeps track of all elections. Dam, my wishes are bigger than my thoughts," said Danny.

"Daddy knows, but you know daddy, he only tells, what he wants you to know. He should have been a secret agent." Said Simon

"You got that right!" Danny became silently surprised.

"Well, see you both on Thanksgiving, Delia's helping mama with the dinner." Said Teddy.

After the conference call, Danny and Teddy turned in for the night. It was after 12 midnight and Teddy needed his rest for the games. He hung the do not disturb sign on the door knob outside.

The Money Exchange

Friday, late morning they were up after a good night's rest, with very few words beyond good morning. After they were dress, a rush to the elevator, down to the restaurant for coffee. And whatever else to satisfy Danny's big appetite. Breakfast cutoff was 11:30 am. Molly, had just started her shift. She saw them and rushed over with a smile. They were her first customers; Teddy and Bobby were her last the day before.

"Hey guys, you're on time for a late breakfast, what can I get for you?"

"I'll have coffee and one of those cobblestone muffins."

"And you my friend?" She smiled, asking Danny.

"Molly, I'll have coffee, and the biggest turkey sandwich you can find with all the works, and a tall glass of water."

"Give me a couple of minutes." She hesitated, looked at Teddy, and asked,

"What do I call you?"

"I'm Teddy, this is Danny, why the interest?" He asked.

"Well, I have information that I'm sure you'll be interested in. We'll talk in a few."

Danny looked at Teddy somewhat confused,

"Do you remember her from our last time here? She must have just started working."

"No I don't. She seems ok. We'll just hear what she has to say, and take it from there."

It took her about 5 minutes to return with a full tray with everything they ordered. They began to eat and talk about home and Thanksgiving dinner for, it must have been two or three hours. Anything about the family was time consuming. Molly was waiting for a good time to talk to them and needed their full attention. She had served her last customer and a break when she went over to their table.

"Okay guys, here's the story. Danny, how well do you know Sheena?"

"Just Sheena, one of the finest bitches on the circuit," he said.

"Sheena is Bobby's big sister. They're the children of Boryenka Fedorov, a wealthy Russian crime boss in Vegas.

"What? That's about the best info of the day, right Danny?"

"So we're being played," said Danny.

"No Danny, its information we can use. Molly you are a true friend."

"I hope you guys don't find trouble. None of this came from me, ok?"

"Don't worry I didn't hear a word you said. I have to meet the little runt at 4pm." said Teddy.

He looked at his watch, it was 3:40. "Danny, you can pay the lady, and again, be generous."

He gave Molly another 100, and suggested she do as she did before, because this time it was well deserved.

"Well Molly, I don't know when we'll see you again, but it's nice to know you're here."

Teddy was reluctant in telling her when they were leaving, and always keeping one step ahead of the game. What he and Danny had heard about the Russians was good, but trust can come at a very high price.

He and Danny headed for the bar. Danny without question walked with his brother, looking around to see if he could spot Sheena but without any success. Before they could set down Bobby showed up. Danny for the first time met Bobby, and wasn't impressed by the little Russian. Bobby was sporting this time, a gold colored baggy suit. Teddy was thinking, this guy must have a hard time shopping. He would do better in jeans.

"Bobby, this is my brother Danny."

Bobby made no attempt to hug Danny and with good reason. Danny was too big, and too tall. He handed Teddy a briefcase and said, "It's all there, you want to count it?"

"Tell you what Bobby, I'm going to trust you." He handed Danny the briefcase.

"I'll see you in 48 or 72 hours."

"Happy birthday Teddy," said Bobby."

"How did you know about my birthday?" Teddy asked.

"Your brother thinks a lot of you, and with great respect. Wish I had a brother like that. I've heard that he likes one of the girls here, I believe her name is Sheena."

Teddy wouldn't elaborate, and continued with the exchange.

"Where do we meet for the payoff?"

"Here, take this number, put it in your phone. It's the paid in full call, 724-346-3855. After 48 hours I will call you, if you don't answer the interest goes up after another 24 hours. My suggestion is, you answer the call. Now, what's your number?"

Teddy gave him his cell number and motioned Danny to go to the elevator. They walked away and into the elevator. As soon as the doors closed Danny couldn't hold his curiosity any longer.

"Teddy what's in the case? Or should I ask how much is in the case?"

"One hundred grand my friend!"

"This has got to be your last straw, as I see it we are riding on a half million dollar," said Danny.

The elevator door opened, they stepped out looking up and down the hall before heading for their room. With that kind of money they rushed hurriedly to key the room and secure the money. Teddy immediately went into the bedroom, checked the bathroom, and the closets. He scanned the rooms to see if anything was disturbed. So far everything met his approval.

He said to Danny, "I want you to take the elevator to the fifth floor, that's the floor to the garage. Walk down through the garage down to the street. Walk away from the front of the casino. Flag a taxi and go rent a car. I'll stay here with the money. Drive the car back to the fifth floor. If you can park it close to the elevator, do it. We're leaving Saturday morning. It's almost 6pm. I'm going down to the tables at 8, so make it as quick as you can, and be extra careful, no distractions please."

Was this the omen for Teddy? And the time to break his habit and addiction that would someday be a failure to the family? As he counted the cash delivery from Bobby it was all there, 100 grand. He didn't need the money. Molly had given him a chance to change his mind with the information about the Russians. Was this the greed of Teddy, or the greed of chance?

There was no way that he and Danny would return to Vegas. They were not soldiers with arms, and would never challenge the Russians on their own turf. Teddy never packed a gun in his life, and Danny's size was the only threat to anyone.

If lady luck was to be, today was the day. Teddy waited for Danny to return with the rental. To him, it seemed like a minutes became an hours, and holding such a large sum of money away from the tables, made him very nervous, without Danny.

Danny was back with time to spare, as he arrived, and as cool as Teddy has ever seen him.

"All done my man, I rented an Escalade so we can dash in style," he said.

"Sure Danny, and draw all kinds of attention, couldn't resist huh?"

Teddy has never owned a car. He believed that living in the city of Chicago, he didn't need any mechanical responsibilities. Danny of course, was a freak for mobility, especially if it had four wheels. His preference was the largest Cadillac made, second to the stretch limo. It would be at the airport when they arrived back in Chicago.

It was almost 8pm, and the time Teddy was scheduled to make his appearance in the casino. He gave Danny his plans in detail.

"I'm going to leave the money with you, and not under any circumstances are you to open the door for anyone, especially

Sheena. We can't trust these Russians. I'm almost sure when she see that I'm alone, she'll come up to find you. Didn't think I didn't know she was here yesterday, right?" He smiled.

"Man, you're good!" Danny said.

"Daddy didn't raise a fool," said Teddy.

"I won't need any of that cash. I'm going to use the escrow that I set up. When I double the winnings I'll cash out. No sleeping Danny. They're not going to like it when I take the money and run. The last straw has got to be the big one."

"Good luck, but I don't need to tell you that."

"We'll take shifts getting a good night's sleep, and checkout in the morning. No, let's change that, I'll call from the airport and checkout."

The casino had never experienced habitual gamblers like Teddy. For years he gambled, and he lost, but he would never leave the casino any given day until he won it all back, and more. But this would be the last time they would see him in Las Vegas.

Teddy cashed out at 500 grand above his escrow. He told the office to make the transfer without delay before he went up to his room.

After a good watchful sleep, at 9am they loaded the escalade. Danny parked in the garage, next to the elevator, and they left for the airport.

Chapter five

They arrived at O'Hare airport at 3:30pm, Chicago's time where they rushed to find Danny's CTS luxury Cadillac. Danny was glad to be home. He drove straight to his condo in the inner city. His place was an auxiliary to Teddy's CPA business and storage for records of the family estate, and 5 minutes from the office. Arriving at 4:30 pm, they made their way in Danny's place keeping a watchful eye on their surroundings. When they entered the condo Teddy went to Danny's room that had a safe embedded in the interior wall, and into a closet with a weight of approximately 500 pounds. He opened it and placed the money, still in the attaché case. The money would remain out of sight, and out of mind.

Teddy was glad to be home in Chicago, four days before Thanksgiving and dinner with his family. Teddy didn't worry about the Russians and if the timing was right he had plans to shake them.

Monday would be the 48 hour deadline to make the call to Bobby for the payoff, and he had to make his move. He picked up the phone that was connected to the business, the condo landline where all calls were forwarded and recorded weekly messages. The first message was from Benny.

"Hey Teddy, this is Benny, I got robbed man! They busted my back door and took some of my best equipment. I've got to talk to you man! I called you Friday. It must have happened after I closed Thursday night. Give me a call soon as you get in."

Benny was the owner of Benny's Pawn Shop, one of the largest pawn shops in Cook County. Teddy had warned him several times about upgrading his security. Benny was a tight wad, and didn't like to spend money, but he was one of Teddy's clients.

Message 2……. "This call is for Nathan Bishop, Mr. Bishop this is Sarah from the county's land records office of zoning, and building permits. I'm calling to sadly inform you that Leman Flannigan has passed away, with a longtime illness. He left you a note after he completed your recordings that said, he hoped that he would have time to see you again, and your phone number. You can pick them up anytime, Monday thru Friday, 8am to 4:30pm. Thank you, and have a nice day."

It had been almost three months ago when Teddy asked Leman to show records that the family house extended the basement upwards, eliminating the living footage. This was only to show of record. Leman had told Teddy of his illness, and how his medical bills were stacking up because the insurance didn't cover everything.

The opportunity was good for Teddy, and he'd paid off all of Leman' outstanding medical bills. He never asked Leman if he had any family because his family wasn't the problem. He had given his office Teddy's number to keep him informed.

Message 3........"Mickey here..... Hey Teddy, you need to come down when you get a chance I've got some new inventory you've just got to see. Tell Danny I've got some that he will flip over. See you when ever." The machine clicked. "End of new messages."

Mickey Vaughn was the owner of Pandora's Jewelry, and a longtime client, one of Danny's favorite jewelry stores.

Danny was in the kitchen and heard the 2nd message. "Who was that guy that died?" He asked.

"Remember when I told you I was working on getting blue prints to show that the basement of our house had no basement. Daddy asked me if it was possible. I told him anything's possible."

"And you found this guy at the rezoning office." said Danny.

"The timing was good, mission accomplished. We'll pick up the records on Monday."

"Man I am so glad that mama and daddy don't have life threatening illnesses like that. Have they ever talked about any health problems? Daddy would tell you if he did, right?" asked Danny.

"For the longest time Daddy would only talk to me about his special room and that's what we worked on for years. He must have stocked that room with food to last for a year."

Danny picked up the phone, but this time to check the bank's balance on the family's account. He did a check every weekend to satisfy every transaction and deposits. The account's final readings were $6.351.010.00. This included everything coming in from their two brothers and little sister. Danny was more than satisfied and told Teddy. The interest on the account itself would put the family into new found wealth without investments. And Teddy, the masterminded CPA, would do well giving up his addiction.

They spent the rest of the evening watching TV, and making plans for the week. On Sunday they went to the community fitness room for a workout, suited up for a Chicago cold winter afternoon, and jog a five mile run through the city, greeting the on lookers they knew well.

Monday's drizzling snow with a forecast of 1 to 2 inches didn't slow the business schedule of a short week. Three days before Thanksgiving and into 24 hours past the 48 hour deadline for the loan payoff call.

Around 9:30am they made their first stop at Benny's Pawn Shop. He must have kept his eyes on the front door looking for them, and opened the door with a smile, and relief. He immediately told them to come to the office, a small room under lock and key in the rear of the store. He told one of his clerks where he would be. After telling Teddy and Danny what he had lost, Teddy reminded him of his last conversation with him about security. Danny asked him if he thought it was an inside job.

"I have to trust my guys, what else can I do? Anybody that you hire you have to trust them, I can't run this big place all by myself."

"Benny I'm going to make a suggestion and it's only a suggestion. You need to spend some money and put in a silent alarm directly to the police. Get rid of that loud bell that only tells the thieves they have to leave. You can get a security system that has 5 or 6 Cameras you can put all over the store and a recorder in your office. Report your losses to the insurance company. If they don't replace your losses, then go to another company.

"It's almost **2016** Benny, hello! Didn't you learn anything from George Bush, Freedom comes with a price of peace, and peace ant here yet! We're in the new world order. Don't worry so much about spending the money, it's the end of the year, and you can write it off. That's my job."

"Man, why didn't I think of that?" said Benny, as he scratched his head.

"That's why you hired me, remember?"

They returned to the front of the store. Danny had no interest in buying from a pawn shop but Teddy was looking at some of Benny's cell phones. They were part of his new inventory that wasn't taken. "Hey Benny, how much are your cell phones?" He asked.

"That's a bargain, only $29.95 each, when you finish using them you can toss them, and they can't be traced. Why would you need phones like that Teddy, don't you have your own service?"

"Danny and I are cutting off a lot of our out of town business, and bringing it all back to Chicago. We figure that we might have an overload, and we have to be in more of a **premeditated** function to accommodate the family. I'll take two, what do I owe you?"

"Don't worry, it's on me for the good advice," said Benny.

"I'll be in touch, don't forget my suggestions, and don't waste time, Benny."

They left the store at 11:30am; the next stop was Pandora's Jewelry, cross town, close to Teddy's office. The last stop would be the county office. Teddy had learned never to stop at any government office at lunch time. The wait would be at least two hours or more.

Danny didn't waste any time getting to his favorite store. It was just a visit to check out the new inventory Mickey had, and kill two or three hours. They had an excellent business relationship with all of their clients and never missed the chance to extend their courtesy.

"Hey Mickey, what's up, heard you had something good." said Danny.

He was busy with a customer, and Danny started to browse the show case looking at the new medallions, and men diamond rings. He had never given up on fashion jewelry after leaving the grid iron days.

"What do you think Danny, sweet huh!" said Mickey.

"I'll take one of each... just kidding man. This is nice, let me think about it," said Danny.

Danny never made hasty decision, it ran in the family, and Mickey knew that. Teddy could see that Danny was really going to think about it from the gleam in his eyes at the precious stones.

"So Mickey.... How's business? Sounds like you're in good spirits," Teddy asked.

"Can't complain Teddy, thanks to you getting my books straighten out."

"You told me that your office is close by if I ever needed advice."

"It's was about 7 blocks on Clark Street, the next street up, and across from the **Chicago Hilton Hotel**. Or you can just give me a call, you have my number."

After browsing a while longer, they bid farewell to Mickey, and on to the county office. Danny waited in the car, and told Teddy to make it quick.

It was 2:30 and they left for Danny's place to fix lunch, and remain the rest of the day. They were never big on eating out, and both love to cook. When they arrived Teddy called their mother and father, as they normally did if they were not out of town.

His mother answered the phone. "How's my girl doing today?" he asked.

"Well it's about time you called. I haven't talked to you since last week."

"I know, and I'm sorry. I love you. Where's daddy?"

"He's outside, something about a truck. A man delivered a truck with his name on the papers and said it was his, got his name on the tag too. Did you do that?"

"You and daddy deserve everything we can get for you. You both are the greatest."

"Well then, where's mine? Delia took that 40 year old VW when she went off to school. She loves that car and will never give it up. Don't worry about me son, I don't need a car as long as I have your father. I know all of you mean well. I am so proud of my children. You all are my lifetime gift. Here's your father, tell Danny don't forget Thanksgiving we've got plenty of food.

"Hey son, when did you decide to get me a new truck? I love it, and it's my favorite color. Things must be doing well."

"We love getting things for you and mama. You've worked so hard for all of us. Oh, by the way, I picked up the blueprint for the house, no more possibility, it's done."

"I'm sure your mother reminded you of Thanksgiving dinner, Delia will be here on Wednesday morning. Thanks son, and tell the rest of the boys, I love them."

"I've already talked to Simon and Michael and they're on their way, I'll see you Thanksgiving. Tell mama I love her."

Two days before Thanksgiving, and Teddy made the call to Bobby. There was never any conversation between him and Danny about the money in the safe. He told Bobby that he wasn't coming back to Vegas, and he would have to pick up the money. Bobby was surprised and confused, because now he had to tell his father.

"I'm coming for you man, that's right, I'm coming to Chicago." He hung up, and Teddy was not surprised.

Red Square Gambling Circuit

Boryenka Fedorov had a small office in a back room of Mandalay Resort & Casino with a Russian cuisine, on the Las Vegas Blvd. south strip, and close to the Blackjack Casino. He met with Bobby and Sheena when Bobby called him about his problem. Boryenka had never had this problem before with his soldiers for any payoffs. He could see the fright in his children when they entered his office. He began with swift and stern embarrassment for them.

"This guy from Chicago, what do you know about him? You told me, you watched him for a long time."

"Daddy he was a big spender."

"I've never seen a gambler like him. And he would win every time he came to the casino. He had crowds around him every time. Sheena spotted him when she hooked up with his brother. He was always with him, like he was watching every move his brother made."

"Then how did you approach him?"

"I didn't exactly approach him at first. I found his room number and left a note for him to meet me that night."

"What? A note, you left him a note." he yelled.

"You left him a note, like you're some little love starved bitch, stupid, so stupid."

He turned to his daughter.

"And you Sheena, I heard you balled the big guy. What did you get from the reamer, probably nothing that made any sense, what so ever."

"When you met him how much did you offer?" he asked Bobby."

"I offered him 50 grand, and told him the payoff would be 5% on top of the fifty to be paid in 48 hours, and another 5% after 72 hours."

"And what did he say?"

"He said, why not 100 grand? He seem like he got a little upset."

"Was anyone around to maybe, hear the conversation?"

"No not really, there was only the waitress, and she wasn't really there." said Bobby.

"Oh ....she was there, and heard everything, dummy! I'm going to tell you about this Teddy, his brother, and the family."

"His name is Nathan T. Bishop, they are known as the first family of Chicago. There's not a lot to find outside of the family, because it is, what it is, a family. This guy Teddy was named after his father. He's the accountant that handles all the money in the family. The brother is an ex-football player. They have two brothers, a marine captain, and the other, a congressman and lawyer in Washington D.C. The younger sister is a doctor, so I've heard, and can be as dangerous as her brothers. When you offered Teddy money, you pissed him off. He doesn't need money, and you gave him a chance to get free money. These people don't frighten easy. The one call Teddy, he's got a new way of doing business. I've heard that all of his clients, he put them on a flash drive. He's probably got all of Chicago's corrupt police on a flash drive, the mayor, and the governor. Molly, at the restaurant she lowered the boom on you and Sheena. Now they know who you are, and pissed them off more." Sheena stood up from her nervousness of hearing what was about to take place from her father, and begin to rant in denial.

"I'm not going to Chicago, Bobby was the one that gave away the money. I did my part."

"Yes, just like the little whore you are. You are my daughter, but I would never pay a 100 grand for a piece of ass."

"You can kiss my ass for a 100 grand." She stormed out of the room.

"Did you hear that little bitch disrespecting her father?"

"You'll leave for Chicago Wednesday morning, okay? Boris and Milka will go with you."

They were two of Boryenka's heavy hitters, and security for his son. "Daddy I don't get up until afternoon, I'm at the casino until 3 AM." said Bobby.

"I don't care what time you leave, just get my money. I don't want to see you until you have my money, and tell that sister of yours to get rid of the attitude."

Chapter Six

Delia received a call from her big brother Teddy early Tuesday morning. She was always excided hearing from him. Every call was like the first in a long time. She talked to all of her brothers every month but he was calling to confirm that he had talked to daddy, and that she would be home Wednesday the day before Thanksgiving. She was ready to leave that same day and was on the road by evening. Teddy and Danny only lived 10 minutes away from their parents and never lived outside of Chicago. Simon was a regular visit for Delia when she visited Martin in New York. He had a law firm in the city and doing well.

When Delia finished medical school, she applied for a resident Pediatrician at Children's Hospital in Philadelphia, and lived there since. At age 29 she still remembered the excitement of getting married to Martin, but after postponing the wedding they remained friends.

Before her brother Michael, the youngest of the boys and closest to Delia had moved back to the east coast from his station in California she would fly out to visit him. He trained his sister in martial arts, and how to shoot fire arms. Hand guns and rifles. She advanced to a marksman and sharpshooter. Philadelphia wasn't the safest place to live, and Michael shipped the two special handguns at her request, using the secured armed forces mail delivery system. Michael now lived in Virginia.

Since she was a teen in high school she had always driven the now 40 year old 1976 Beetle her mother gave her for graduation. She was always a happy kid, and very popular in high school. Life was filled with love and the joys of having a close family.

On the trip home she remembered growing up on the dead end road. At the time it was called Amberstone Road. It was a dirt road and the only house setting at the end of about a quarter mile.

The address was One Amberstone before the Government's political correctness changed it to 1953, the year that her daddy was born.

The house set kind of on a hill. She would play up and down the road, and her brothers played football all summer long into the winter months. The road was widened, and it became two, with a center median lawn with four trees. Her house was the largest in the community when three houses were built on each side of the road. Then the road was paved, and named Amberstone Court. There were neighbors and everyone began to feel like a part of a community. The court was a proud community, one way into a circle bend, and one way out. Delia had an expression of where she lived to her friends, directing them to the "**Horseshoe's Bend**," of the house on the hill.

Her mother started a beautification club with the neighbors. They would meet in the spring of every year to decide what to do for the neighborhood. Everyone would plant flowers in their yards. Emma Jean would plant lilies in five different colors that represented her five children. She called them, "The Lilies of Amberstone."

The community was a scenic view of welcome, and the summers were showered with daises, tulips, and so many wild flowers. Like a plane had dropped millions of seeds everywhere.

In the evening Delia remembered going into her parent's room facing the court, chatting with them while they were in bed. She could see the horseshoe's bend when the street lights came on, and see all of the neighbors when they arrived home from work. Sometimes she would count them until she fell asleep.

When she arrived that late morning, the day before Thanksgiving, the Chicago streets were covered with two inches of snow from a storm moving down from Canada, and a forecast threat of at least a foot on Thanksgiving Day.

As she drove down the one way into the horseshoe's bend she noticed the curtains from the upstairs bedroom of Sarah and Charles Logan were pull back, the last house on the left at the end of the court. She knew that could only be Sarah. She was the good neighbor, and longtime friend of the family. She always kept a close watch on the neighborhood. Delia casually waved knowing Sarah was somewhere in the window.

Sarah was a housewife, same as her mother, but they never had any children. Charles worked at the same GM plant as her father, but a few years behind him.

When she pulled up to the house she saw her daddy's new truck and the personalized plate with the family name Bishop. She began to smile, catching a glimpse of her mother who stood inside behind the closed front door screen.

When she parked, not wasting any time she leaped from the luggage filled VW, dressed in a slightly oversized navy peter jacket, fatigues, and deep combat boots, onto the porch as she raced to embrace her mother. With every visit she packed her VW as though the stay would be longer than expected. Only four months had passed since she last saw her parents but the next time always felt like the first time. She had never given up the habits of changing clothes at least three times a day since high school. Shopping in the mall was her personal addiction, and a revolving expense for her parents when she was growing up. But they didn't care, anything for their little girl.

"Hi mama!" she said. The door swung open as she kissed her mother on the lips.

"Hello honey, look at you! You're dressed like your brother Michael, with all that marine stuff on. You must be tired from that long drive. Come on in, your father and I've been waiting."

"Nathan your daughter's here."
Nathan was in the family room watching the world news. One of his daily habits after working his special room, he called it, keeping an eye on the world, and what the second term of the president might have to say for his state of the union speech.

"So, how's the doctor been since the last time? Are you taking good care of the children?"

He was proud of what his daughter had become, and how much she loved caring for children.

"Everyone's doing fine daddy, considering the conditions. The most important thing is, I love being there for them."

Emotions were always uncontrollable when Delia talked about her kids at the hospital. She would sometimes tear up.

"From the way you're dressed looks like you've been spending a lot of time with your brother Michael. What tall tales has he been filling you with?"

"No tales daddy, he's just teaching me how to protect myself."

"Well, he would be the one to do just that."

"Honey, are you hungry? You must be starving. I can fix you something," said Emma Jean.

"I'm okay, just need to stretch a little."

"Not to change the subject," said Nathan.

"But, can I borrow Delia for a while? I have something to show her."

"Well, honey here it comes, go with your father."

Nathan took his daughter's hand and led her to the pantry. He opened the door and all she could see was wall to wall food, and a small table he moved back toward the front door. He closed the door and turned on a small light just above the table.

When Emma Jean began to get comfortable in the living room, and wait for Delia and her father's return, the knock at the front door wasn't a surprise. She assumed that the snow had slowed down Sarah's timing to come over. She had made her way up the hill to see Delia, and to accommodate her usual neighborly noisiness.

When Emma Jean opened the door Sarah was breathless trying to find words of reason.

"Where's my little Delia?" She asked.

"It's your auntie Sarah." She yelled. Hoping Delia would hear her call.

"Sarah, she's with her father upstairs. It's going to be awhile. They have a lot to talk about."

Sarah moved to the bottom of the stairs with intentions of going to find Delia, ignoring Emma Jean. Emma Jean grabbed her arm, telling her not to disturb them, and not wanting her to find out she had intentionally misguided her.

"Don't be so impatient, Sarah, you'll see her, it's not like she just stopped by for a quick visit."

"Are you sure?"

"Trust me, mother knows best. Don't forget Thanksgiving. The boys will be here too. You and Charles can see everyone at the same time."

The Logan's were invited for dinner because Sarah and Emma Jean had grown to be very close over the years, and the closest of the neighbors to the Bishop family.

But Sarah and no one else outside of the family knew about the special room, and never would. Friendships were never to be indulged in the privacy of the Bishop family.

"Okay, I'll see you tomorrow? Do you need me to bring anything?" She asked.

"No... just you and Charles. When you see the boys cars you can come over, you're a good friend, and neighbor Sarah, we love you," Assuring her of her good will.

"Tell Delia, welcome home........again!"

Emma Jean watched her friend as she went down the hill, but not before peeking into Delia's car, looking back at Emma Jean, as she watched her nosey friend. The snow had picked up a steady flaking to show the tracks of Sarah's small feet back to her house, and to the window of her domain.

Delia and her father were unaware of the knock at the door, and the grand entrance of Sarah. The entire pantry was sound proof, one of Nathan's last minute designs. They continued their journey

53

with Delia's amazement. Her father had reached in behind the rear shelves of canned food that covered the back wall. The shelf was more than a foot deep. He pulled on a lever and the whole wall moved open to the swing of a door. Delia's mouth widen when she saw a down stairs behind the big door. Her father motioned with a hand of welcome.

"Ladies first," he said. Delia smiled and moved toward the steps. There were six steps in a comfortable slop, and a sharp left turn to the entrance to the full living quarters that he'd created for his family.

Delia was amazed beyond words and held her silence for more than minutes could describe as her father watched her walk around the room, a special room with the same sq. footage as the original foundation, and a gigantic living area of enormous proportion. There was an entire wall filled with canned food, the same as the pantry. At the end of that wall was a free standing portable upright cabinet for dry good storage. The storage space was about six feet tall. The height of the room itself was more than six feet to satisfy the movement of Danny and Michael, the only ones who towered more than six feet tall.

There were five portable cots with thick mattresses and heavy bedding that set in the middle of the room. Delia was still speechless as she moved around. Her father just followed her with a smile.

On one of the walls there were four solar powered generators with four cables leading to the outside, and onto the roof, where four solar panels were mounted on the roof, two facing the east and two facing the west. Delia wouldn't know this until her father explained it, and the reason.

Her curiosity grew stronger when she noticed a closed door and the entrance to another room with more space framed in a corner. She opened the door to find a fairly large bedroom with a queen size bed, a full bathroom, closet, and a dresser.

What was really extraordinary about the special room, the entire area of each wall was a cushion of an asylum structured for injury protection. All of the four walls were framed with a fire retardant shield, and six inches deep. The ceiling was a hanging structure of the same.

Finally she couldn't resist the temptation of so many questions, and the need for her father to explain the purpose of the special room.

"Daddy, I can see that this room was meant to be for living, but for who, and why? Is this for us, the whole family? How did you do all of this?" she asked.

"It wasn't just me. Your big brothers Danny and Teddy were the ones who made everything what it is, with still more to come, at least that's what they keep telling me. They're going to bring their whole operation here. They call it an electronic ghost in cyberspace, with an encryption of all the accounts they have." He began to scratch his head, as though he was wondering what was to come next.

"Daddy it looks and sounds like a fairy tale that came true. Like some of the stories I tell my children at the hospital. To them, the words I spoke became a reality of truth," she said.

Nathan held his daughter's hand, but before directing her to the stairway he placed a fine tooled wooden box in her hand. She didn't know when or where he picked up the box. He told her it was a gift from his past, and something that was long overdue. She opened the box to find a pair of what looked like brass knuckles but she noticed they were iron. Something a father would give his sons. She asked, what were they for, and why would he give them to her? He told her that maybe Teddy, one day would tell her the story.

He removed one of the knuckles from the box.

"Here try it on. Your hands are small like mine and should be a perfect fit." he said.

"Philadelphia's not a very safe place to live and a single woman should be able to take care of herself. I know your brother Michael has taught you a lot, but the more you prepare yourself the better."

"It's getting late, let's go upstairs and see what mama's got for lunch," he said.

Emma Jean had found her way to a comfortable spot on the sofa, and cuddled for a nap after Sarah went home.

Awakening from her light slumber of footsteps on the hard wood floor Delia shouted with a gesture of surprise...... "Caught yah, taking a nap huh!" she said with a smile. Her mother stroked her eyes.

"Mama you must be tired, without even checking to see what you've prepared for Thanksgiving," she said.

"Almost, just a few more things I'll need for the salad." She stretched from the quick snooze.

"Mama, I had planned a trip to the mall. I can pick up whatever you need."

"Oh no honey, your father can run that errand for me. The snow is still coming down and I know he wants to try that new truck of his in the snow."

"You know how I am about the mall it's been a few months since my last visit. There's a market on the way, so, what do you need?" she asked.

"Well if you insist, I keep forgetting you're a big girl now. I'll make it easy; I need everything for the salad, and two nice pies. We're having nine settings for dinner."

"Your birthday was two weeks ago, and I didn't forget. I have some gifts for you, so you won't mall shop and buy the same things. Just have a seat and get comfortable. You and daddy enjoy yourselves while I run upstairs."

"Your mother is something else. She spends a lot of time preparing for you," said Nathan.

"Nathan, can you give me a hand with the packages please?"

"I'll help you, ma, hold on."

"No honey your father will help. You stay right where you are."

Nathan rushed to give Emma Jean a hand at the top of the stairs. She had four packages, and was trying to hold on to the fifth one.

"You're always trying to carry more than you can handle."

Delia waited patiently. Watching her parents doing something they'd always enjoyed, made her happy.

"Now honey, I want you to open all of them. Make sure we got the right of everything. I'm not going to tell you or give any hints. Now open."

"Your mother's more excited than you are, don't you think?"

"She's been like that for as long as I can remember."

Delia opened the first package, and to her surprise it was an under armor suit. The second package was another under armor, one black, and the other one was red.

"Mama, why did you buy two of the same thing?"

"How can I forget, you've always changed clothes like a movie star getting ready for the next scene. Keep going, open the next one."

Delia began to get more and more excited as she rushed for the next gift.

"I wish the guys were here. We should have waited for Thanksgiving Day for this!" she said, as she ripped the paper from the third gift. It was a jogging suit, and one more of the many she had. A notebook and a doctor's medicine bag with a stethoscope, and thermometer inside were the third and fourth gifts. The front of Delia's shirt was drenched with tears and for that moment she decided to try and change all of the excitement. She thanked her parents for all of the love and joy they have given her and the life they'd made for her.

"It's after 6 o'clock and I think I'd better get going with the errands and my mall stop."

"Honey why the mall? Can't that wait until another time? Like black Friday, the day after Thanksgiving."

"No mama, my brothers will be here and I'm not going shopping while they're here."

"It's just a few things that can only be found at the mall."

"When I leave I'll be going straight to New York. Martin and I are going to a heritage ball and I need to shop for an Afro wig for the occasion since I shortened my hair, and of course I need a nice evening dress so I can swing my stuff."

"Honey, get going so you can hurry back before the snow gets too bad. We'll wait up for you.

Chapter Seven

Around 7:25pm of that same evening Delia went shopping. Bobby arrived at the O'Hara airport along with Boris and Milka. They were to pick up Teddy's address from a downtown pool hall and bar owned by another Russian in Chicago, and the friend of Bobby's father. They didn't know the only address they would find listed was Teddy's fathers address on Amberstone Court, and the only address for the Bishop family. Bobby didn't know anything about Chicago and this would be his first time in the city. He and the two goons rented a car with navigation. Bobby was the only one who knew how to read a map. He was born in America.

After picking up the Bishop address from the bar they checked into the Hilton Hotel where they would decide what time they would pick up the money from Teddy. The hotel had only the penthouse available. $1200.00 a night was of no concern to Bobby. He was only thinking of collecting his father's money.

It was after 9 o'clock but the late hour wasn't of any importance to him, just getting the money back at any cost.

At 9:40pm he called Teddy's number to let him know he was coming for his money. There was no answer from Teddy's number. Bobby could only think of what his father would do if he returned with no money.

At approximately 11 pm Thanksgiving eve a 911 call was placed by a caller reporting that three suspicious men were seen entering the residence at 1953 Amberstone Court, gun shots rang out and 15 minutes later the three men hurriedly leaving getting into their car and speeding off. The call placed was from a neighbor and close friend of the Bishop family. In less than two minutes the street was filled with marked police cars, sirens blasting and emergency lights.

For the next two hours, a Chicago community would experience crimes of retribution of non-other than perfect murders beyond any shadow of doubt. The entire neighborhood resident's lights went on like a Christmas tree. Everyone filled the street, and the one family friend waited nervously for Delia to return from when she had seen her leave earlier.

The police circle the house before they attempted to go in. The lights were on as they rushed in with guns drawn. The neighbor rushed out of her house and ran as fast as she could to follow the police. After five police entered they found two bodies lying close to each other with no movement.

The neighbor entered and began to scream seeing her friends lifeless, lying in a pool of blood.

After calming herself but still tearful, she said, "Oh my God, Emma Jean!" One of the officers asked.

"Who are you?"

"Mam, why don't you wait outside for her please, we'll get a statement from you as soon as we get the detectives here."

"My name is Sarah Logan, I'm the one who called you. Their daughter must be on her way home, I saw her leave earlier."

Charles, Sarah's husband was a very sound sleeper and didn't hear any of what was going on outside. Sarah rushed in to wake him, hoping he could help her break the news of her parent's death.

"Charles, Charles wake up, I need to talk with you!"
He immediately noticed a nervousness in his wife's voice, and knew something serious was upsetting his wife.

"Nathan and Emma Jean have just been murdered!"

"What? How do you know this?"

"I saw the whole thing, well I didn't see them getting murdered, but I saw three men going into the house and I heard gun shots. I called the police when I saw them going into the house, that's why they were here so fast."

"I didn't hear anything!"

"Of course you didn't, it would take a dirty bomb for you to wake up!"

"Charles I saw Delia leave earlier and its getting late. She's got to be on her way home."

"How do you know that? She could be over her brother's house."

"Tomorrow's Thanksgiving and she's always home with her mother and father. Let's go outside, I've got to catch her before she sees her parents."

At 12:20pm another unmarked police car and coroner's van pulled up to the front of the Bishop's house to take the bodies away. One of the officers pointed toward Sarah and her husband standing outside directing a plain clothe detective that just arrived. As he approached them he introduced himself.

"Good evening, or should I say good morning, my name is detective Lt. Niles Heller from the Chicago police department, and your names?"

"My name is Sarah Logan and my husband Charles, I was the one who called 911 when I heard gun shots!"

"And what time was this?"

"It was 11 o'clock, and we're still waiting for the daughter

"When do you expect her?" Ask the Lt.

"At any time, I saw her leave around 9 pm. She must have went shopping, that's the only reason she would leave so late. I saw three men rushing from the house around 10:45 after I heard the shots."

"Mam, how were they dressed, could you see what race or maybe how tall were they?"

"They look like and average height but one was kind of small in height, almost like a boy!"

"And what kind of car were they driving?"

"Oh, smaller man was driving, and it was a big car, like a limousine."

"Well, the officers are starting to leave, and the coroner will take the bodies down town for further examination. Mrs. Logan, you continue to watch for the daughter, and I'll leave an officer here just to secure the area until later this morning. We'll continue the investigation and I will need to talk to the daughter."

"Should I call you when Delia, that's her name.....call you when she gets in? It is thanksgiving!"

"It doesn't matter mam, here's my card. Keep calling until you get me."
Sarah and her husband waited and watched from their front window for Delia's return. At 3am they were getting sleepy and went back to bed. Delia never arrived.

Bobby and his two associates, after the killing of Teddy's parents, waited at the hotel's penthouse trying to figure out what to do. Bobby stared to drink the vodka he had started to drink before they went to the Bishop's house. And one of the reasons why everything got out of control that led to the killing.

"Ah man! He said, this is bad! I don't know what to do." As he took another drink.

"If you didn't pull the piece everything would be fine! Where did you get the gun anyway?" Asked Boris.

"We were only to collect money from Teddy, and the old guy said, Teddy didn't live there!" said Milka.

"I got it from the guy at the bar to protect myself. Anyway, the old lady came after me, and the old guy picked up something."

"He said, Teddy didn't live there man!"

"He said that when you asked, is Teddy in? And then you forced your way in! Can you blame them? Tell that to your father."

"You don't even know if Teddy knows his parents are dead. Now he's coming after you!"

"You mean us!" Said Bobby.

"What do we do now?" Boris asked.

"I don't think we have but one choice, and that's wait for Teddy to call!"

The End of Part One

Part Two, Premeditated 2020
(The Supreme 13, will publish in 2016)

The Truth of Life as a Conservative and Patriotic Family.
Lamar Paul Jones served his country from 1940-1953
Married DeElla Jackson 1938, 1st son 1939, 2nd son 1941

Forever Lasting Love, R I P

Only the son knew his Mother Dear as a Conservative Cherokee-Black, and Patriot of the country she loved so much.

Living in Washington's District of Columbia, she completed training at the Opportunities in Industrialization Center May – August and awarded a Diploma in Testimony as a keypunch operator, Washington, D.C. 1976.

As a volunteer Activist she was awarded a certificate of recognition for community service. 1979.

The Government of the District of Columbia presented her with a certificate for participation in The Senior Citizen's Club. 1987.

Superior Court of the District of Columbia, Certificate of Appreciation, May 1979.

Miss me – But let me go.
DeElla Jones 1920 - 1990

Let's Make America Great Again

Henry Jackson Born 1860 – DYINK. Conservative Native Cherokee-Black American of Athens, Georgia, and worked as a Railroad Porter.

Delia Jackson, Born 1862 – DYINK. Married to Henry Jackson 1878, The conservative Black American house wife

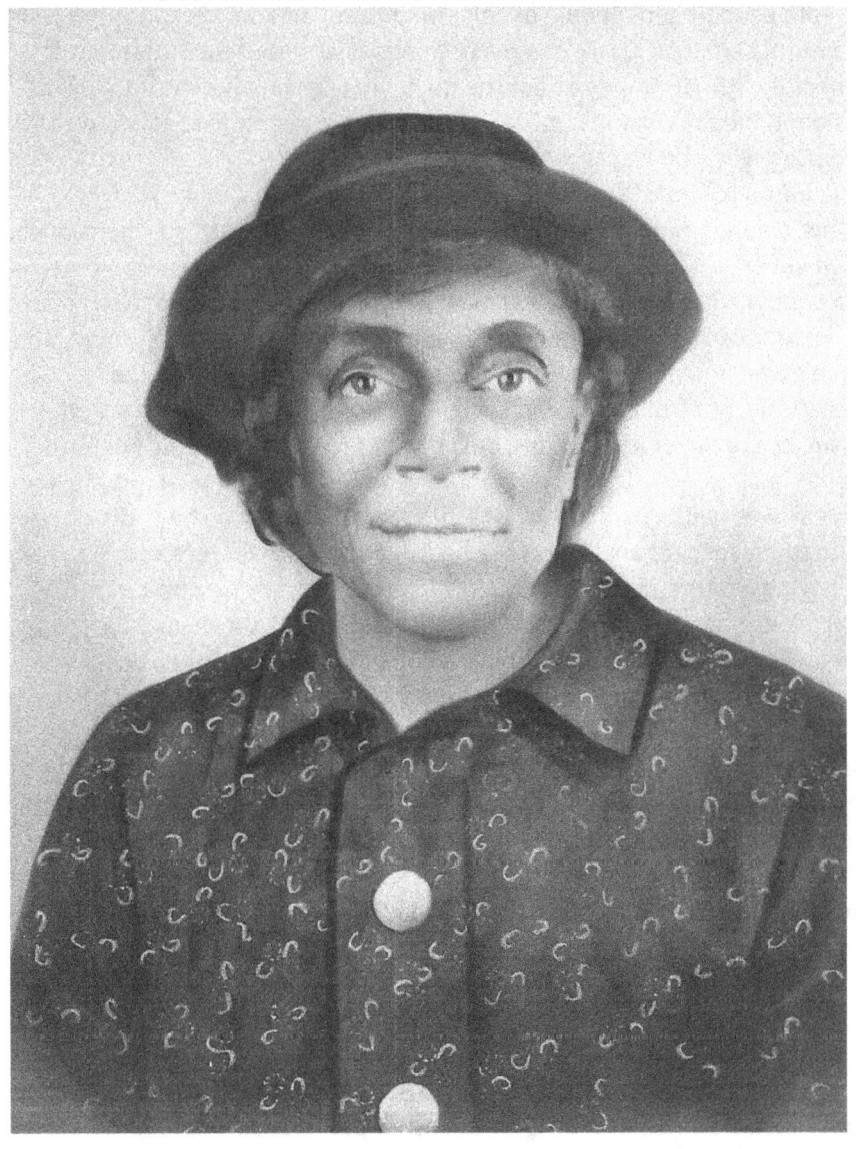

People in Power

Of the many ways, when people, especially people in power, separate or segregate people of color or culture, and only because of color or cultural behavior. To try and make things clear about the statement a Democratic senator made about the qualifying light skin color of the now president, Barack Obama 2012, and not having a Negro dialect, when only expressed when he wants too.

As a black American, seventh generation, with a dark skin from Athens, Georgia, since I was very young and growing up in a southern town, I have never had what the senator calls, a Negro dialect. And at the time I didn't know what a Negro dialect was! My question is, and was, what does the senator call a Negro dialect? One would only think that in his mind, and with his age, and being white, he was segregating the speech as being racially different from his English language, and thoughts of segregated racism. I have never like to write or speak of race. Thanks to my English teacher, a black American of ten or twelve generations, she taught me how to speak well, with character, and clearly. The dialect that I have did not relate to my race, or any sound she heard, and she never referred to me as not having a Negro dialect. And according to the senator, I don't qualify to be president because my skin is too dark. I know now the dialect the senator speaks of, but his ignorance can only relate it to what he calls a, "negro dialect." If he would only listen closely to the great Martin Luther King Jr's speech, he will hear only the ownership of the dialect of a man speaking with, and the ownership of his words. This was a man of character that spoke to people, and for people and it didn't matter what the dialect or skin color. The tone was genuine and not separated by a race, and not referred to as one. And the tone was not separated by the color of skin but the integration of people. The owner's dialect spoke with character that only this man could present it.

I hear the now president, Barack Obama, and the race baiters like Al Sharpton and Jesse Jackson, and the way the president subscribe to their ownership with words.

Mr. Obama, a first generation African American, has learned how to be a rock star. He has mastered the art of public speaking as he was taught to present himself. And so have many lawyers and politicians for decades. Yes he was taught! Words are power, but for an extraordinary speaker, if you are lacking the human side of dignity and truth, you are left without emotion, and only the mocking of great speakers of deceitful dialect.

I love a good speaker and the president is one of the best in his own words I've heard in many years. His dialect was his own, and had everything to do with race, and separation. The senator used the words of, "without a Negro dialect, and with the light color skin." His words of a qualifying African American for president.

Many years have passed, and the president's tone, and words of a legacy have fallen into the history of our country, and the people are the victims to his words of deceptions. I find myself listening to the echo of his words, and almost in tears when he speaks. I wait for something other than the pose of disappointment and deception. Something to tell me, that I was wrong, for not voting for him, but it never happened. I can only feel that my choice was right for myself. It was my moral belief from the beginning that this man was, and is morally deceptive. I remain, one of the happiest people in the world for my moral decision. I no longer listen to this president of the United States 2015. And for the many years, the gray in the president is beginning to show as do his mind. The days of spring and summer on the white house lawn, Mr. Obama will wipe his brow, and the liberal media will not have the field day of a cosmetic cover up, but a cover up, and not to unveil the stress of the worst job of any American president. Because, liberal begets liberal! In this country we will never rid ourselves of race baiting as long as we have race cultures we question, and a government to confuse us. The senator has the mind of separation and segregation.

And in my mind ....."Senator, there is no race related dialect or color of skin that makes any man a better man, only the man of character as he stands, can make himself a better man."

Clifford H. Jones, Author

Let's Make America Great Again

The Truth

It is the final of belief that never ever needs.
It is the end of how, and not make hearts bleed.
It brings a smile, of relief and faith of not to ponder.
The truth can never carry on, a doubt of do I wonder.
The truth...... is the end, of what will always be.
To tell it now, and you can the truth will set you free.

Promises to Keep

In this place I trouble myself, like no end to a horrid dream.
But to know who, that I am, and know just where to lean.
I walk like a lion so bold, and ever so sleek.
For I am in this world, but not of this world,
Because of promises to keep.
Like the wings of an eagle, I soar to heights unknown,
The distant climb is never too steep.
To save my soul at heaven's door, with all the promises to keep.